A Wayne in a Manger

GERVASE PHINN

PENGUIN BOOKS

PENGUIN BOOKS

Published by the Penguin Group
Penguin Books Ltd, 80 Strand, London WC2R ORL, England
Penguin Group (USA) Inc., 375 Hudson Street, New York, New York 10014, USA
Penguin Group (Canada), 90 Eglinton Avenue East, Suite 700, Toronto, Ontario,
Canada M4P 2Y3 (a division of Pearson Penguin Canada Inc.)
Penguin Ireland, 25 St Stephen's Green, Dublin 2, Ireland
(a division of Penguin Books Ltd)
Penguin Group (Australia), 250 Camberwell Road,
Camberwell, Victoria 3124, Australia (a division of Pearson Australia Group Pty Ltd)
Penguin Books India Pvt Ltd, 11 Community Centre,
Panchsheel Park, New Delhi – 110 017, India
Penguin Group (NZ), cnr Airborne and Rosedale Roads, Albany,
Auckland 1310, New Zealand (a division of Pearson New Zealand Ltd)
Penguin Books (South Africa) (Pty) Ltd, 24 Sturdee Avenue,
Rosebank, Johannesburg 2196, South Africa

Penguin Books Ltd, Registered Offices: 80 Strand, London WC2R ORL, England

www.penguin.com

First published by Michael Joseph 2005
Published in Penguin Books 2006

031

Printed in Great Britain by Clays Ltd, St Ives plc

ISBN-13: 978-0-141-02688-6
ISBN: 0-141-02688-X

www.greenpenguin.co.uk

For my parents
Margaret Patricia Phinn
and Richard Joseph Phinn
who never missed a Nativity
in which I took part

ILLUSTRATIONS BY CHRIS MOULD

PENGUIN BOOKS
A Wayne in a Manger

Gervase Phinn is a teacher, freelance lecturer, author, poet, schools inspector, educational consultant, visiting professor of education – but none of these is more important to him than his family.

For fourteen years he taught in a range of schools, then acted as General Advisor for Language Development in Rotherham before moving on to North Yorkshire, where he spent ten years as a schools inspector, time that has provided so much source material for his books. He is a Fellow of the Royal Society of Arts and an Honorary Fellow of St John's College, York.

Gervase Phinn lives with his family near Doncaster.

Acknowledgements

The majority of these stories appeared originally in my Dales books. However, for this collection I have embellished here, embroidered there, so the versions here tend to be a variation on the originals.

Two teachers mentioned in the text use stories by Nicholas Allan and Susan Wojciechowski: 'A Night to Remember' is based on the story *Jesus' Christmas Party* written by Nicholas Allan (published by Random House Children's Books), and 'The Woodcarver' is based on *The*

Christmas Miracle by Susan Wojciechowski (published by Walker Books).

Of the poems, 'Nativity Play' first appeared in *The Day Our Teacher Went Batty*, and 'Christmas Lights' and 'Christmas Presents for Miss' in *It Takes One to Know One* (both books published by Puffin Books).

Contents

I

A Very Special Time of Year

December sunshine, bright and brittle, shone through the classroom window and lit up the vicar. His sparse sandy hair shone like gold, his small black eyes sparkled and his cheeks shone as if they had recently been scrubbed.

'This is a very special time of year, children,' he said jovially, addressing the infants who stared up at him with open mouths. 'Can anyone tell me what it is?'

'Christmas,' volunteered a small wiry boy with a feathery fringe, who began waving his hand in the air like a daffodil in a strong wind. 'It's Christmas.'

'It is indeed,' agreed the vicar, smiling beatifically. 'It's Christmas, and a very, very special time of year.'

'I'm gerrin a bike,' the boy told him.

'I'm gerrin a doll what can wet 'er nappies an' talk,' added a large girl with a round moon face and hair in untidy bunches.

This was the signal for all the children to shout out what presents they were hoping to receive from Father Christmas.

'I'm gerrin a remote-controlled car.'

'I'm gerrin a train set.'

'I'm gerrin a . . .'

'Children! Children!' exclaimed the vicar, raising a hand like a crossing patrol warden stopping cars. 'Christmas is not just about presents, you know. It's really a celebration of a birthday. It's about the birth of a very special baby.'

'I know what it were called,' said the small wiry boy.

The vicar interlaced his long fingers just beneath his chin in an attitude of a child praying and smiled. 'I'm very glad to hear it,' he said in that solicitous and kindly tone often possessed by men of the cloth.

'It were called Wayne,' the child told him.

'Wayne? Certainly not! What a thought!' cried the vicar in mock horror.

'It were!' cried the boy, undeterred. 'Babby were called Wayne.'

'No, it wasn't called Wayne,' said the vicar, his jaw tightening and his voice quavering a little. He bit his lip momentarily. The poor man had imagined that speaking to a group of small children about Christmas would be an easy enough task but he was now regretting he had ever agreed to visit the school that morning. 'The baby was called Jesus,' the vicar told him, slowly and deliberately.

'It were Wayne,' persisted the child, nodding vigorously.

'Jesus!' snapped the vicar.

'Wayne,' repeated the child. 'I know, 'cos we all sang about it in assembly: "A Wayne in a manger, no crib for a bed."'

❄

Of all the activities that take place at Christmas, it is the infants' Nativity play that I most look forward to. Innocent children re-enacting one of the greatest stories of all time capture the essence of Christmas. To see Mary, aged six, draped in pale blue and tightly clutching Baby Jesus (usually a large plastic doll) to her chest, never fails to bring a tear to the eye. To see Joseph, a thick multicoloured towel draped over his head (usually held in

place by an elastic belt with a snake clasp) and attired in a dressing gown and red socks, always brings a sympathetic smile to the lips.

Then there are the shepherds (usually a motley group of little boys who scratch, fidget and pick their noses throughout the performance), the Three Kings (who invariably forget their lines or drop the gifts), the adoring angels clad in white sheets with bits of tinsel stapled to the bottom and uncomfortable-looking cardboard wings strapped to their backs and, of course, there's the grumpy Innkeeper, who very often steals the show.

There is something very special and heartwarming about the infant Nativity.

2

The Infant Nativity Play

*E*very teacher of young children has a story to tell about the Christmas Nativity play. There was the time the Innkeeper, when asked if there was any room in the inn, answered, 'Plenty', and ushered the startled Holy Family inside; the occasion when Mary dropped Baby Jesus, immediately bursting into floods of tears as the large pink doll rolled off the stage; the time that the Archangel Gabriel informed

Mary that he had tidings of great joy to bring but had completely forgotten what they were; and the memorable moment when the giant cardboard star, which had been suspended on a wire above the stage, fell on Joseph who, very much out of character, rubbed his head and exclaimed, 'Bloody 'ell!'

❄

Then there was the time when the little boy playing Joseph strode confidently onto the stage and asked the small figure in blue who was cradling her baby, 'And how's our Jesus been today, Mary?' 'He's been a right little so-and-so!' came the blunt reply.

In one school I eavesdropped on a conversation between the Headteacher and a parent concerning the Nativity play the children were to perform. 'So what's this play about then?' asked the mother in all seriousness.

In another school I heard a father complain that, 'Tha allus do t'same play every Christmas. Tha wants to do summat different!'

❄

As an Inspector for English and Drama, it was inevitable that I should be invited to attend several school nativities each Christmas. On one unforgettable occasion, at a small school deep in the heart of the Yorkshire Dales, the

Angel of the Lord – an angelic-looking little girl with golden curls and great innocent eyes – appeared on stage. She was draped in a shimmering white nylon sheet trimmed with sparkling tinsel and had elaborate golden wings, cut out of cardboard, attached to her back. She did indeed look the part.

The heavenly child was, however, unaware that the pretty ensemble she was wearing had somehow gathered up at the back. As she approached the front of the stage, little arms outstretched, one of the small shepherds, huddled around an imitation fire, had noticed.

The Archangel Gabriel began: 'Fear not, for glad tidings of great joy I bring –'

'I can see your pink knickers!' the shepherd informed her in a whisper so loud it could be heard at the back of the hall.

The angel continued regardless. 'To you in David's town this day, a baby boy will be born –'

'I can see your knickers!' said the shepherd even louder. 'Chardonnay, I can see your pink knickers!'

The Angel of the Lord, screwing up her little face angrily, turned around sharply and told him to 'Shut yer gob!' before continuing her speech in the most innocent of voices.

Things improved until the arrival of Mary and Joseph, both in thick woollen robes and headdresses. The heaters in the hall blasted out hot air, the bright spotlights shone down

on the cast relentlessly and the small actors
began to blow out their cheeks, huffing and
puffing, scratching and fidgeting. As the

Three Kings presented the happy couple with
their gifts, Mary sighed and thrust the large
doll representing the Baby Jesus, with a fair bit

of force, on to the lap of Joseph with the words, 'You 'old Him a bit. 'E's gerrin dead 'eavy!'

As I approached a Dales school one December afternoon, I found all the children heading for home. I stopped a small boy loaded down with Christmas cards, calendars, decorations, presents and all manner of boxes and bags as he tried to negotiate the narrow gate.

'Where's everyone going?' I asked. 'There's a Nativity play here this afternoon, isn't there?'

He stopped for the amount of time it took

to tell me bluntly, 'It's off!'

'It's off?' I repeated.

'Aye,' he replied. 'T'Virgin Mary's got nits!'

3

The Visit of Father Christmas

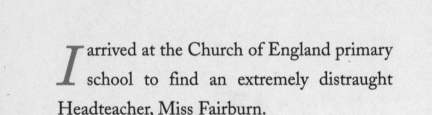

I arrived at the Church of England primary school to find an extremely distraught Headteacher, Miss Fairburn.

'Oh dear, Mr Phinn,' she gasped, 'oh dear me!' Teachers are sometimes rather nervous when I arrive in school but I had never had such an effect before. This woman was near to fainting. 'Oh, it's not you, Mr Phinn. It's just that Father Christmas has appendicitis and it looks as if we will have to cancel the party. The children will be so disappointed. They were so looking forward to it.'

It turned out that Father Christmas was Mr Beech, the school crossing patrol assistant, who every year took on this arduous role at the infant and nursery Christmas party. However, he had been rushed to hospital after breakfast and his daughter had telephoned to say that he would not be able to oblige as Santa Claus that afternoon. I am quite sure that there were tears in the Headteacher's eyes. 'The children will be so disappointed. They are all so excited about Father Christmas coming.'

What could I do? I was the only available man. Nervously I donned the costume, and after a strong cup of coffee entered the hall to find row upon row of open-mouthed, wide-eyed children. They squealed in delight when they saw the familiar red coat and fluffy, white cotton-wool beard. Everything went pretty well until a bright little spark announced loudly, 'You're not real, you know.'

'Oh yes, I am!' I replied in a deep, jolly Father Christmas voice.

'Oh no, you're not,' she persisted. 'Your beard's held on by elastic. I can see it. And Father Christmas has big boots. You're wearing shoes.'

'That's true but I got stuck in a snowdrift on my way here and my boots were so filled up with snow that I borrowed these shoes from

Mr Beech.' School inspectors have to think on their feet when it comes to bright little buttons like this one.

'You can't have because Mr Beech has gone to hospital,' continued the child. 'My mum told me because he lives next door. You're not the real Father Christmas!'

'Oh yes, I am!' I said in my loud, jolly voice and heard a whole school hall shout back: 'Oh no, you're not!'

The Headteacher intervened and bailed me out by starting the singing. After three verses of 'Rudolf the Red-nosed Reindeer', each child came forward in turn to receive a small present.

'What are the names of your reindeers?' asked a little boy.

'Well, there's Rudolf,' I started, 'and Donner and Blitzen and er . . . er . . .'

Miss Fairburn, seeing that I was struggling, helped me out again by explaining that Father Christmas was rather deaf.

'Some of the snow from the snowdrift is still in his ears,' she said.

One child asked me if I knew her name and when I replied that I didn't, she looked crest-fallen. 'But I thought Father Christmas knows all the boys' and girls' names?'

Miss Fairburn explained that Father Christmas's eyes weren't too good either and he had such a lot of letters to read.

One rather grubby little scrap asked if she could sit on my knee.

'No, Chelsea,' said the Headteacher firmly. 'I don't think–' She was too late. The child had clambered up and was clinging to me like a little monkey.

'Get down, Chelsea,' said Miss Fairburn loudly. 'I don't think Father Christmas wants children on his knee. He's got a poorly leg.' Any more ailments, I thought, and I would be joining Mr Beech in the Royal Infirmary.

'Now, you be a very good little girl and sit on the floor, Chelsea,' I said in my jolliest voice, 'otherwise all the other children will want to climb up.' Chelsea stayed put and held fast like a limpet. I chuckled uneasily until the child's teacher at last managed to prise her off. The Headteacher shrugged and looked knowingly at the teachers standing around the hall.

After the children had sung me out to 'Jingle Bells' I was invited into the staff room. It was extremely hot under the red suit.

'Father Christmas, you were a great hit,' said Miss Fairburn. The staff looked on and nodded. 'And we'd like to give you a little Christmas gift.'

'Oh no,' I said, 'it really isn't necessary.'

'Oh, but I think it is necessary,' insisted the Headteacher and presented me with a small bottle-shaped parcel which looked as if it had been rather hastily wrapped in some bright red tissue paper.

I shook my gift and held it to my ear. 'After-shave?' I enquired. 'Is it after-shave?'

'No, Father Christmas,' the staff replied as one.

'Is it a little bottle of whisky?'

'No, Father Christmas,' they chorused.

I tore off the wrapping to reveal a small brown bottle of medication. The label read: 'For infestation of the head.'

'Chelsea's just got over head lice,' said the

Headteacher. 'It's not advisable to be too close to her for the time being.'

'And she's just recovered from scabies,' piped up a beaming teacher. The rest of the staff then joined in with a hearty 'Ho! Ho! Ho!'

4
Storytime

❄

'It was cold and dark that December night many, many, many years ago, and on the hillside, where the icy winds whistled through the dark trees –'

'I can whistle, Sir.'

'And the grass was frosted and stiff with cold –'

'Do you want to hear me whistle, Sir?'

'Not now, Dominic, thank you. Perhaps

later. Listen to the story, there's a good boy. Matthew, the little shepherd boy, huddled in a dry hollow with his sheep to keep warm. The cold winter wind blew about his ears, and high above him the dark sky was studded with millions of tiny silver stars –'

'Miss Stirling gives you a silver star if you do good work.'

'It wasn't that sort of star, Dominic. These were like tiny diamonds sparkling in the darkness. This was the night that a very special baby would be born.'

'Jesus!'

'That's right, it was Jesus.'

'I've heard this story before. I know what happens.'

'We all know what happens, Dominic, and we are going to hear what happens again.'

'Why?'

'Because we are. Now, soon, a very special baby would be born and His name, as Dominic has already told us, would be Jesus.'

'Was He induced?

'Pardon?'

'Was Baby Jesus induced?'

'No, He wasn't induced.'

'I was induced.'

'Well, Baby Jesus wasn't induced.'

'How do you know?'

'Well, I know because it was a long, long time ago and they didn't induce babies then.'

'Why?'

'Because they didn't. Just listen to the story, Dominic, and then we will all find out what happens.'

'But I know what happens.'

'Well, we're going to hear what happens again!'

'Sir?'

'Yes, what is it, Elizabeth?'

'What does seduced mean?'

'Oh dear,' I sighed wearily, catching sight of the teacher attempting to hide her laughter behind a hand. 'I will tell you another time – when you are older. Now, let's get on with the lovely Christmas story. And then amidst the tiny diamonds that sprinkled the dark sky there appeared a great shining star, a star that sparkled and gleamed with such a wondrous brilliant light that –'

'How much did He weigh?' asked Dominic.

'Who?'

'The Baby Jesus.'

'I haven't got to the Baby Jesus yet.'

'I was an eight-pounder. My granny said I was like a plucked turkey when –'

'Dominic!' I said very quietly and slowly. 'Now just listen to the story. You are spoiling it for all the other children.'

'But I know how the story ends,' he replied undaunted.

'Then why don't you come out here and tell it to us, Dominic,' I said, throwing in the towel.

And so he did. Like a seasoned actor taking centre stage, he came out to the front of the class and recounted the Christmas story in such a simple, animated and confident way that we all listened in rapt silence.

'Once upon a time there was a man called Joseph and a lady called Mary and they were friends and they played games together and they had fun. Then they had a wedding and after the wedding they went home and then they had some lunch and a drink and then they set off for Beth'lem on their honeymoon and they went on a donkey. When they got to Beth'lem there was no room at the inn so they had to stay in a barn round the back and then Mary had a little baby and she called it Jesus

and she put Him in a manger and all the animals were around Him and the big star shone up in the sky and then the shepherds all came and then the Three Kings came and they all gave Him presents because it was His birthday and Baby Jesus had plenty of milk because there was lots of cows about.'

There was silence at the end of Dominic's story, then he looked at me and said, 'OK?'

'OK,' I replied, 'very OK.'

On my way out that morning a little girl with long blonde plaits and an angelic face approached me shyly. 'I liked that story,' she said quietly.

'Did you?' I replied. 'I'm glad. Thank you for telling me.'

'But Dominic tells it better than you do. Happy Christmas!'

5
The Grumpy Innkeeper

*T*he little actor in one version of the Christmas story that I attended looked very disgruntled. I heard later that the lead part of Joseph had been given to another child and the would-be thespian had not been too pleased. He had argued with his teacher to no avail, and still wasn't very happy when he was given the role of the Innkeeper.

'But why can't I be Joseph?' he had persisted.

'Because you can't!' the teacher had snapped, 'and if you don't stop whingeing, William, you'll end up as a palm tree.'

On the night of the performance, Mary and Joseph arrived at the inn and knocked loudly on the door. The Innkeeper, who had remained grumpy all through the rehearsals, opened the door with a great beaming smile.

'Innkeeper! Innkeeper!' Joseph began. 'We have travelled many miles in the darkness and the cold. May we come in?'

'She can come in,' the Innkeeper said, pulling Mary through the door, 'but you can push off!'

The voice of an exasperated teacher in the wings, 'No, no, you silly boy!' brought proceedings to a halt. A moment later Mary emerged from the inn to join her bemused spouse and they headed for the stable downstage where a large pink plastic doll representing Baby Jesus sat propped up in the manger.

The doll, of the modern talking variety, had a mop of curly blonde hair and a round pink face. When Mary picked it up, the movement started it off, and in a loud tinny American accent, it announced: 'My name is Tammy. Are you my mommy? My diaper needs changing.'

Mary, with great presence of mind, thrust the doll under the imitation hay saying, 'Nightie-night. Time for a little sleep.'

❄

The infant children had been asked to illustrate the Christmas story. One small paint-spattered child had produced a large and very colourful effort full of adoring shepherds, kneeling kings and assorted animals gathered around the crib.

'What's that in the middle of your picture, Amy?' asked the teacher, indicating a large white ball resting in the manger.

'The egg,' replied the child.

'Egg?' repeated the teacher, puzzled.

'You know, Miss,' explained the child, 'the egg that Baby Jesus hatched out of.'

'Baby Jesus didn't hatch out of an egg!' chuckled the teacher. 'Whatever gave you that idea?'

'But you said He did,' replied the child, her forehead creasing into a frown and her bottom lip beginning to pout.

'When did I say that Baby Jesus hatched out of an egg?' enquired the teacher.

'You said, "Mary laid Baby Jesus in a manger,"' replied the child.

6
Nativity Play

❄

O h Miss, I don't want to be Joseph,
  Miss, I really don't want to be him,
With a cloak of bright red and a towel on my
  head
And a cotton-wool beard on my chin.

Oh Miss, please don't make me a shepherd.
I just won't be able to sleep.
I'll go weak at the knees and wool makes me
  sneeze

A Wayne in a Manger

And I really am frightened of sheep.
Oh Miss, I just can't be the landlord,
Who says there's no room in the inn.
I'll get in a fright when it comes to the night
And I know that I'll let Mary in.

Oh Miss, you're not serious — an angel?
Can't Peter take that part instead?
I'll look such a clown in a white silky gown,
And a halo stuck up on me head.
Oh Miss, I am not being a camel!
Or a cow or an ox or an ass!
I'll look quite absurd and I won't say a word,
And all of the audience will laugh.

Oh Miss, I'd rather not be a Wise Man,
Who brings precious gifts from afar.
But the part right for me, and I hope you'll
*   agree,*
In this play — can I be the star?

7
The Visitation

One December, I was invited to a Nativity play held in a school in one of the few industrial towns in my area. Joseph, a rather fat boy dressed in a Mexican poncho and a towel over his head, did not look entirely happy when he heard the news of the imminent arrival of the baby.

'Are you sure about this?' he asked, an anxious expression suffusing his round face.

'Course I'm sure!' Mary replied. 'An Angel of the Lord told me.'

'Are you sure it was an angel?'

'Course I'm sure. Her name was Gabrielle.'

Hearing this, I remembered that the school was very big on equal opportunities.

'I think I'm going to faint,' Joseph sighed.

'Pull yourself together. It's great news. Angel Gabrielle told me not to be frightened.'

'I'm dead worried about this, Mary,' Joseph confided, shaking his head solemnly. 'It's come as a big shock.'

'There's nothing to worry about, silly. Everything will be all right.'

'I suppose we'll have to get married then.'

46

'S'pose so.'

'Are you sure you're having a baby, Mary?' Joseph persisted.

'Yes, I've told you, and we're going to call Him Jesus and He will be the best baby in the whole wide world and we will love Him very, very much and take care of Him.'

Joseph nodded but still didn't look too happy. 'All right then,' he sighed.

How many young couples, I thought to myself that afternoon as I watched the small children act out their play, had been in that situation?

❄

47

At one little primary school, deep in the Dales, I attended an unforgettable Nativity play which was improvised by the children. This is not always a good idea because small children can be very unpredictable, particularly when faced with an appreciative audience.

Mary, a pretty little thing of about six or seven, was busy bustling about the stage, wiping and dusting, when the Angel of the Lord appeared stage right. The heavenly spirit was a tall, self-conscious boy with a plain, pale face and sticky-out ears. He was dressed in a flowing white robe, large paper wings and sported a tinsel halo, somewhat crooked. Having wiped his nose on his sleeve, he glanced around suspiciously then sidled up to Mary, as a dodgy market-trader might, to see if you were interested in buying something from 'under the counter'.

'Who are you?' Mary asked sharply, putting down her duster and placing her hands on her hips. This was not the quietly spoken, gentle-natured Mary I was used to.

'I'm the Angel Gabriel,' the boy replied with a deadpan expression and in a flat voice.

'Well, what do you want?'

'Are you Mary?'

'Yes.'

'I come with tidings of great joy.'

'What?'

'I've got some good news.'

'What is it?'

'You're having a baby.'

'I'm not.'

'You are.'

'Who says?'

'God, and He sent me to tell you.'

'Well, I don't know nothing about this.'

'And it will be a boy and He will become great and be called – er, um . . . –' The boy stalled for a moment. 'Ah – called Son of the Most High, the King of Kings. He will rule for ever and His reign will have no end.'

'What if it's a girl?'

'It won't be.'

'You don't know. It might be.'

'It won't, 'cos God knows about these things.'

'Oh.'

'And you must call it Jesus.'

'I don't like the name Jesus. Can I call Him something else?'

'No.'

'What about Gavin?'

'No!' the angel snapped. 'You have to call it Jesus. Otherwise you don't get it.'

'All right then,' Mary agreed.

'And look after it.'

'I don't know what I'm going to tell Joseph,' the little girl said, putting on a worried expression and picking up her duster.

'Tell him it's God's.'

'OK,' Mary said, smiling for the first time.

When the Angel of the Lord had departed

Joseph entered. He was a cheeky-faced little boy dressed in a brown woollen dressing gown, thick blue socks and a multicoloured towel over his head, held in place by the inevitable elastic belt with a snake clasp.

'Hello, Mary,' he said cheerfully.

'Oh hello, Joseph,' Mary replied.

'Have you had a good day?'

'Yes, pretty good really,' she told him, nodding theatrically.

'Have you anything to tell me?'

There was a slight pause before she replied. 'I am having a baby – oh, and it's not yours.'

8
The Woodcarver

One of the great delights of being a school inspector is being able to sit in at Storytime and see the small children's upturned faces, their wide eyes and open mouths, as they hang on every word uttered by the teacher as she lifts the story from the page.

The story Mrs Webb began reading that afternoon was a most moving account about a woodcarver. This man had been a happy, good-natured person until his beautiful wife and young child had died. Then he ceased to smile and became bitter and unpleasant to anyone who came near him.

One cold winter's day, however, shortly before Christmas, a widow and her small son called on him and asked him to carve a set of Nativity figures. 'I had some as a child,' the woman told him, 'but sadly I have lost them. My father carved them for me and I thought that by some miracle they would turn up.'

'There are no such things as miracles,' the woodcarver replied gruffly. 'I have no time to carve them for you.'

The widow pulled her young son close to

her. 'Please,' she said, 'my son will be so disappointed.'

Looking at the gentle up-turned face of the boy, the woodcarver relented. 'Very well,' he told her, 'I will carve your figures.'

The next morning, there was a little knock at the woodcarver's door and, opening it, he found the young boy there.

'May I sit and watch you carve the figures?' he asked.

It was very cold outside, so the woodcarver grumpily agreed. He sat the boy down by the fire, and told him to keep quiet. As the old man deftly carved the figures of the Three Kings, the shepherds, the angels and even St Joseph, the boy noticed that their faces looked so mournful, as if they had suffered some great tragedy.

'Why are your faces all so sad?' he asked. 'When you come to carve Mary's face, please make her smile. She's just had a new baby and would be very happy.'

The woodcarver laid down the figure of a shepherd he was carving, strode to the door, and ushered the boy out. 'I told you not to speak,' he said curtly.

The next morning, however, the boy returned to the woodcarver's house and was again settled down next to the fire.

Mrs Webb arrived at the most poignant part of the story, pausing to ensure that she had the children's full attention.

The woodcarver tried again and again to carve the faces of Mary and the infant Jesus but without success. 'I cannot make her smile,' he muttered.

There was soon a little pile of discarded carvings on the floor. The man finally reached into a drawer and took out a charcoal sketch of a young woman sitting in a rocking chair, cradling a tiny baby. It was of his wife and child. With tears streaming down his face, he carved the face of Mary in her rough woollen shawl, looking down lovingly at her precious baby.

At this point, Mrs Webb stopped reading and a tangible silence fell on the classroom. She put her hand to her face and began to cry. I was at a loss what to do. Never, in all the years

I had been observing teachers, had I ever seen a teacher break down like this in front of her class. She took a handkerchief from her pocket, dabbed her eyes and continued to weep.

'I'm sorry,' she sobbed. 'I'm sorry, I just can't read any more . . .'

I felt a lump come into my throat and my eyes began to fill up, too. Then a small boy stood up and made his way to the front of the class. He took the book from the teacher's hand, gently patted her on the arm and said, 'You sit there, Miss. I'll finish the story.'

At break-time I sought out the boy. He was in the playground, sliding with his friends on the icy surface.

'What you did today,' I told him, 'was a noble deed.'

He looked up at me with a completely innocent face. 'Pardon, sir?'

'It was a very kind and thoughtful thing to do, helping Mrs Webb out like that.'

His smile stretched from one ear to the other. 'Oh, that,' he told me cheerfully, 'I often have to do it.'

9
The Crib

Crompton Primary School was an enormous straggling structure on three levels. The school had originally been built in the late nineteenth century as a Board school to meet the educational needs of children of all ages: infants on the ground floor, juniors on the second and seniors on the top. It now catered for a large population of primary-aged children who lived in the dark and brooding northern industrial town of Crompton. With its shiny brick walls, greasy grey slate roof, small square windows, towers and turrets and enveloping high black iron fence, it resembled a prison or a workhouse more than a school. This could have easily been the setting for a Dickens novel. One could imagine little Oliver Twist standing by the great iron gates or Scrooge scuttling past the row upon row of dark, mean back-to-back terraced housing, drab feature-less warehouses, rubbish-strewn wasteland, on his way to his cold cramped office.

The teaching staff had endeavoured to make the interior of the ugly building as colourful and Christmassy as possible and had decorat-ed the walls in the gloomy entrance hall with huge red cut-out figures of Santa Claus and prancing reindeers, snowmen and Victorian carol singers. A rather droopy Christmas tree stood in a corner.

In the infant classroom, the children were busy colouring Christmas cards. Amidst the sea of faces I noticed Matty observing me from his desk in the corner of the room, a truculent expression on his little face. I felt certain he remembered me. I certainly remembered him.

On my last visit to the school, I had come across this small grubby six-year-old with a tangle of greasy hair and a pallid face. He was a sad, neglected and troublesome boy who had left a lasting impression upon me. 'Do you know, Mr Phinn,' the Headteacher had said to me, 'the poor child got nothing last Christmas because his mother told him that Santa had run out of presents by the time he got to their house.'

On that last visit I had attempted to read the infant children a story but it had been interrupted consistently by a very loud and voluble child called Tequila. At the very front of the classroom now sat the child in question with her plump face, frizzy hair tied up with a bow and great wide eyes.

'Just put your pencils down for a moment

please, children,' said the teacher, 'and look this way. Do any of you remember Mr Phinn, the school inspector? He came into our school earlier this year.'

'I know who 'e is,' said Tequila. I thought it wouldn't be long before she made her presence felt. 'It were 'im what told us about that cat.'

'That's right,' I said. 'Lazy Tom. I read a story to you all.'

'We might be gettin' another cat for Christmas,' Tequila told me now.

'I thought your granny didn't like cats,' I said.

'She dunt, but she dunt live wi' us any more. She's in an 'ome.'

'Well, I am very sorry to hear it,' I said.

'My dad's not,' said the child. 'He said it were best place for 'er. Mi granny dribbles in her knickers and she – '

'Yes, you told me before,' I said quickly.

'That's enough now, Tequila,' said the teacher.

'But I were tellin' 'im about mi granny.'

'Yes, I know you were,' said the teacher sharply, 'and we've heard quite enough. Now, I'm sure Mr Phinn would like to see our crib.'

'Very much,' I said.

The crib was a large but extremely sorry-looking affair with dull strips of wood stuck together haphazardly, scraps of faded hay and huge figures, which had clearly seen better days. The white paint had flaked off the Baby

Jesus giving Him an unhealthy grey appearance. Joseph had lost an arm and the angels their haloes, the Three Kings looked like down-and-outs, while the ox and the ass were chipped beyond recognition. Someone had tried to brighten up the Virgin Mary by repainting her with long yellow tresses, bright red lips, crimson cheeks and an electric blue cape. She had a strange, rather alluring smile on her face. Looking at her now, the adjective 'virgin' was the last word that came to mind.

'They've gorra much nicer one in

Fettlesham,' Tequila informed me. 'Ours is real tatty.'

'But that's what it probably would have looked like,' I told her. 'Baby Jesus was born in a stable, a cattle shed, and He had a manger for a bed. It wouldn't have been nice and clean and bright like the crib in Fettlesham. The stable Baby Jesus was born in would have been full of rather smelly animals and dirty hay. There was no room in the inn, you see, so Mary and Joseph had to stay in the stable and it didn't have lovely furniture and carpets and central heating.'

'Well, they should 'ave booked in advance,' pronounced Tequila. 'It allus gets busy at Christmas.'

'Mary had to have her baby in a cold, dark barn,' I continued. 'He had no nice new clothes, no toys, no cot. He came into the world with nothing. He was one of the poor and mean and lowly.'

Matty, who had been watching with eyes like saucers in his pallid face, shook his head slowly and said quietly but with feeling, 'Poor little bugger.'

No Room at the Inn

Mums and dads, grannies and grandpas, aunties and uncles, neighbours and friends filled the school hall for the Nativity play, the highlight of the school year. I found a seat just as the lights dimmed and a spotlight lit up the small stage.

The curtain opened to reveal the outlines of various eastern-looking houses painted on a backdrop and two rather forlorn palm trees made out of papier mâché and green crêpe paper which drooped in the centre of the stage.

The little boy playing the lead as Joseph entered wearing a brightly coloured towel over his head. He took centre stage without a trace of nerves, stared at the audience and then beckoned a particularly worried-looking Mary who entered, pulling behind her a large cardboard-and-polystyrene donkey.

'Come on!' urged Joseph. 'Hurry up!' He banged on the door of one of the houses. 'Open up! Open up!' he shouted loudly.

The Innkeeper, with a face like a death mask, threw open the door. 'What?' he barked.

'Have you any room?'

'No!'

'You have!'

'I haven't!'

'You have, I saw t'light on.'

'I haven't.'

'Look, we've travelled all t'night, up and down those sand-dunes, through dusty towns, over hills, in and out of rivers. We're fit to drop.'

'Can't help that, there's no room,' replied the Innkeeper.

'And I've got t'wife out here on t'donkey.' Joseph gestured in the direction of a very glum-looking Mary who was staring at the audience, completely motionless.

The Innkeeper remained unmoved. 'And

you can't leave that donkey there. You'll have to move it!'

'Well, give us a room.'

'There is no room in the inn. How many more times do I have to tell you?'

'She's having a babby, tha knaws.'

'Well, I can't help that, it's nowt to do with me.'

'I know,' replied Joseph sighing as he turned to the audience, 'and it's nowt to do with me neither.'

To the surprise of the children there were great guffaws of laughter from the audience.

And so the play progressed until the final magic moment. Little rosy-faced angels in white with cardboard wings and tinsel haloes, shepherds with towels over their heads and cotton-wool beards, the Three Kings in coloured robes and shiny paper hats gathered around Mary and Joseph on the cramped stage to sing 'Away in a Manger' and bring a tear to every eye.

II

Christmas Lights

❄

The lights on the Christmas tree winked
And the snow fell thick and heavy outside.
From the walls of the school hall
Angels spread their silver wings
And the Three Kings held high their gifts.
The lights dimmed and silence fell.
Mums and dads, grannies and grandpas
Stared at the stage expectantly
For the Christmas story to begin.

A spotlight flooded the stage and a small child
   entered.
Wide-eyed, she stared at the sea of smiling
   faces before her.
'Welcome,' she whispered, 'to our . . . to our . . .'

Then she froze like a frightened rabbit
Caught in the headlights' glare.
'To our Nativity!' came the teacher's hushed
  voice off-stage.
'To our . . .' began the child again. 'To our . . .'
'Nativity!' repeated the teacher.
'Harvest Festival!' announced the child.

12

A Night to Remember

There was one particular Nativity play that I remember well. It was held at St Bartholomew's Roman Catholic Infant School and the star of the show was the Innkeeper, played with great gusto by a round-faced little boy of six.

In front of the curtains on the makeshift stage there was a bed in which the Innkeeper was sleeping. He was suddenly awoken by

Joseph banging loudly on the inn door and asking for a room. He clambered out of bed.

'There's no room in t'inn!' he barked.

'Have you nowhere for us to stay?' asked Joseph.

'Tha can go round t'back, if tha wants. There's a barn. Tha can sleep in theer!'

'Is there nowhere else?' asked Joseph.

'No, tek it or leave it. It's all t'same to me. I'm goin' back to t'bed.'

'Righty-ho,' said Joseph, cheerfully. 'Come along, Mary.'

When Joseph and Mary had exited stage right, the cross Innkeeper returned to his bed, stretched, yawned and began snoring loudly.

There was another loud knocking at the

door. The Innkeeper jumped from his bed and stamped his foot angrily.

'What?' he demanded of a group of motley characters in dressing gowns and tea towels over their heads.

'We are the shepherds looking for a baby,' they announced.

'Well, there's no babby 'ere, so clear off! I'm trying to get some sleep 'ere!'

The shepherds departed stage right.

The Innkeeper climbed back into bed, stretched, yawned and began snoring loudly.

There was yet more loud knocking at the door. Once more, the Innkeeper jumped from his bed and stamped his foot angrily again.

'What now?' he shouted, his little hands on

his hips and with a face that would turn milk sour.

'We are the Three Kings come from afar,' announced a small boy swamped in a long red and gold costume. 'We come bearing gifts.'

'For me?' asked the Innkeeper, suddenly smiling.

'No, for a baby.'

'Well, there's no babby 'ere!' the Innkeeper exclaimed, assuming his furious countenance. 'I've just told a lot o' shepherds. Try next door. I'm goin' back t'bed.'

'Righty-ho,' said the first King, cheerfully. 'Come along, you other Kings.'

When the Three Kings had exited stage left, the Innkeeper crawled into bed, stretched, yawned and once more began snoring loudly.

Suddenly a bright spotlight shone on him, lighting up the whole stage, and a crowd of small angels dressed in white appeared and began singing 'Away in a Manger' somewhat untunefully.

'That does it!' shouted the Innkeeper. 'I'm right sick o' this.'

He jumped from his bed, stamped and stormed across the stage to find out what was going on. The curtains then opened to reveal a tableau at the centre of which was a little Mary in blue and Joseph in a dressing gown, white socks and with a towel over his head.

'What's goin' on 'ere, then?' the Innkeeper demanded loudly.

Mary held a finger to her lips. 'Sshhh! You'll wake up the baby,' she whispered.

The grumpy Innkeeper peered angrily into the manger. His expression suddenly changed and a great beaming smile filled his face. 'Aaaaaahhhhh, what a luvverly little babby,' he sighed. 'He's a real bobby-dazzler.'

'Aaaaaahhhhh,' we in the audience all responded as the curtain fell.

13
With Bells On

'Now, if you are all looking this way, children, I am going to tell you the story of Christmas. Now, sit up smartly, nice straight backs, eyes this way, and we will begin. It was a cold, cold winter night many, many years ago when Mary and Joseph arrived in Bethlehem. Joseph walked ahead holding up his lamp to light the way.'

'Didn't he have a torch, Miss?'

'No, Kimberley, he didn't have a torch. There were no torches in those days. Mary was on an old donkey which walked  oh so slowly. Clip-clop, clip-clop, he went. I think he knew that he was carrying a very precious burden that night.'

'Miss, we live next door to Mrs Burdon.'

'This is a different burden, Patrick. This burden was a very heavy weight.'

 'Mrs Burdon's very heavy, Miss. My mum says she's fat.'

'Patrick, dear, just listen. This story has nothing to do with Mrs Burdon. As I was saying, Mary was on an old donkey which walked oh so slowly.

Clip-clop, clip-clop, he went.'

'Miss, I went on a donkey this year at Blackpool. It ran off along the sands and my dad had to chase it. It kicked my dad and tried to bite him, Miss.'

'Yes, well, this donkey was a very special donkey, Dean, a very gentle donkey.'

'Did it have bells on, Miss?'

'No, it didn't have bells on.'

'Didn't they have bells in those days, Miss?'

'I'm sure they did have bells, Dean, but this donkey didn't have any.'

'The donkey I went on at Blackpool had bells on.'

'Yes, well, this one didn't, Dean. Now Mary knew she was going to have a baby very soon.

She had been travelling all day and she felt very, very tired.'

 'Miss, my dad was very, very tired after he chased the donkey.'

'Mary was tired because she had been travelling all day and she was having a baby.'

'Miss, my Auntie Brenda felt very, very tired when she was having my cousin Oliver. She had swollen ankles and a bad back and, Miss, she was always being sick. She said it was the last baby she was going to have because –'

'Patrick, just listen, dear. Mary and Joseph had been waiting so long for the arrival of their very special baby.'

'Nine months!'

'That's right, Patrick. My goodness, you do know a lot about babies!'

'Miss, I know where babies come from as well. My dad told me.'

'Yes, well, this is neither the time nor the place to go into that.'

'Did she go to the hospital, Miss?'

'No, she didn't. There were no hospitals in those days.'

'Miss, my Auntie Brenda had to go to the hospital.'

'Well, Mary didn't. Now, just listen, there's a good boy. My goodness, we will never get through the story with all these interruptions. Joseph looked everywhere for somewhere to stay. He asked at the inn but the Innkeeper said that there was no room. There was only the stable where the ox and the ass slept.'

'Miss, what's an ass?'

'It's a donkey, Dean.'

'I wouldn't like to sleep with a donkey, Miss. The one in Blackpool was really smelly and tried to kick my dad and bite his hand.'

'This was a very nice donkey. Soon Mary would have her very special baby and lay Him in swaddling clothes in a manger.'

'The donkeys in Blackpool were mangy, Miss. My dad said so.'

'I said "manger", Dean, not "mangy". The Angel told Mary not to fear. He brought tidings of great joy but he told Joseph to take Mary and the baby and flee to Egypt.'

'Miss, the donkeys in Blackpool had fleas, Miss. My Auntie Christine was scratching the whole holiday and –'

'I think we will finish the story tomorrow, children. Now, sit up smartly, nice straight backs, eyes this way, and we will wait for the bell.'

14

A Christmas Angel

It was on a cold, raw December day that I visited Bartondale. The sky was an empty, steely grey and the air was so icy it almost burnt your cheeks and ears. The drive from the nearby market town was uphill all the way along a narrow, twisting, slippery road. Barton Moor Parochial School, an austere building of dark grey stone and mean little windows, was surrounded by the bleakest of country. It was set high up above a panorama of dark green hills flecked with snow, deep valleys with long grey farmhouses and a meandering river. Nearby there was a little cluster of houses and an ancient squat church, all surrounded by a fleecy mist. This was the hamlet of Barton Moor.

I was standing with Miss Precious, the Headteacher, staring out of the window in the school hall and across a small playground area, which was covered in a light dusting of snow.

'If an angel were to descend to Earth,' cooed my companion, 'he would surely look like little Jasper.' Standing alone, just beyond the window, was the subject of the Headteacher's observations.

The child did indeed look like a little

cherub: an ocean of golden curls, large dark long-lashed eyes and a pale skin tinged with red on the cheeks. All he needed was a golden halo and a pair of small white wings.

'He's such a quiet, sensitive little boy,' Miss Precious told me in a confidential tone of voice. 'Not a jot of trouble. Always does as he's told, never misbehaves or is silly. But he's so dreadfully quiet. Doesn't say so much as two words all day long.'

'How old is he?' I asked.

'Just six.'

'Most six-year-olds never stop talking,' I said, thinking of the many infants I had met who had a comment to make or an answer for everything.

'But he's not like other six-year-olds,' mused the Headteacher. 'So very quiet and when he does talk he sometimes says the funniest things. He had just started school and was sitting in a large cardboard box in the Home Corner, brumming away. "Are you in your racing car?" I asked him. "No, I'm in a cardboard box," he replied. How I laughed.'

At that moment, the bell signalled the end of break and the children hurried into school, chattering excitedly and rubbing their hands together. Miss Precious and I moved to the front door to greet them. Little Jasper was the last. He stood at the school entrance looking so sad and forlorn, and there on his cheek was a frozen teardrop.

'Aaaahhh, bless him,' sighed Miss Precious. 'Have you been crying, Jasper?' she asked the child.

He shook his head.

'Are you sure?' asked the Headteacher. 'It looks as if you've been crying.'

He shook his head again.

'Look, there's a little tear on your cheek,' she said, gently reaching out. 'Here, let me brush it away.' She swept his cheek with a long finger.

'It's snot,' he told her with a little shrug, and followed the other children into school.

15
Balthazar

Willingforth was something of a show-piece school and Miss Pilkington, the formidable Headteacher, was highly regarded. So I anticipated that the performance would be rather special, and indeed it was.

The school looked particularly warm and cheerful that cold December afternoon. There was just the one large airy classroom. It was impressively decorated - pale blue walls,

navy-blue and cream ceiling beams and sup-
ports, and blue floral curtains. Against the
dominant blues, greens and reds, gold and
silver made the room look very bright and
festive. Using tissue paper of varying colours,
the children had transformed the windows
into the most wonderful stained glass, depict-
ing scenes in the early life of the Holy Family.

On a table in one corner there was a small crib with delicate porcelain figures. In the Reading Corner stood a modest Christmas tree.

For the Nativity play, the desks had been removed and replaced with rows of chairs. By the time I arrived the place was packed with mums and dads, grandparents and governors, all facing a makeshift stage.

Miss Pilkington, a tall, elegant woman, opened proceedings by welcoming everyone. Then the Chairman of Governors, a jolly little man with ruffled hair and crinkled cheeks, read the story of the Annunciation from the Bible in a deep sonorous voice.

As the children sang 'Away in a Manger', Mary, all in blue, entered, accompanied by a small boy in the regulation brown dressing gown. Mary and Joseph knocked on the inn door, found there was no room and were shown to the stable.

Things went like clockwork until the Three Kings arrived on the scene. The first little boy, carrying a golden box and dressed in a red velvet cloak made from curtains, still with the hooks in, and sporting a cardboard crown that covered half his face, announced loudly:

'I am Melchior and gold I bring,
In homage of our newborn king.
I have travelled from afar,
Following yon twinkling star.'

The second King strode on to the stage carrying a blue box. He too boomed out his words:

> *'I am Caspar. Frankincense I bring,*
> *In homage of our newborn king.*
> *I have travelled through the night,*
> *Following yon star which shines so bright.'*

The third King entered carrying a green box. He shuffled nervously to the centre of the stage and stared around him wide-eyed and frightened as if lost in a busy shopping street. The hall was totally silent. The child sniffed, then his small shoulders heaved and great tears rolled down his small red cheeks. Suddenly he let out a most desperate and plaintive cry: 'I don't know who I am.'

'You're Balthazar, Dickie,' Miss Pilkington said in a loud stage whisper, from the side of the room, 'and you've brought Baby Jesus a special present of myrrh.'

'I don't know who I am,' the child whimpered again. 'Please, will someone tell me who I am?'

'Balthazar,' the audience chorused.

'I don't want to do it!' he wailed. 'I don't want to do it!'

The Headteacher moved forward, helped the little boy place the box before Mary and Joseph, gave him a cuddle and, taking his hand, led him off the stage. There was a moment of hush, and then the audience burst out clapping.

16
Christmas Presents for Miss

Chocolates in a fancy box –
For the teacher who is tops!
A tea towel and an oven glove –
From Gemma Thompson with my love.
A bottle stands in thick brown paper,
All the best – from Darren Baker.
Perfumed soap from Lee and Chris,
You're our favourite teacher, Miss.
Flowers in a coloured pot –

A Wayne in a Manger

Happy Christmas, Helen Bott.
A china dog with painted face –
For the teacher who is ace!

And from the nuisance of the class
The Nativity encased in glass.
I know this year I've been a pain,
I'm sorry, Miss – with love from Wayne.

And though she's taught for many years,
The teacher's eyes still fill with tears,
For children know the ones who care
And that is why those gifts are there.

17

The Arrival of the Three Kings

❄

*I*t is often the Three Kings who steal the show, and the highlight of one Nativity was with their entrance. Someone had really gone to town on the costumes for the little boys who came in clutching their gifts tightly; they were resplendent in gold and silver outfits, topped by large bejewelled crowns that shone brilliantly under the stage lights.

'I am the King of the North,' said one little

boy, kneeling before the manger and laying down a brightly wrapped box. 'I bring you gold.'

'I am the King of the South,' said the second, kneeling before the manger and laying down a large coloured jar. 'I bring you myrrh.'

'I am the King of the East,' said the third and smallest child, kneeling before the manger and laying down a silver bowl. 'And Frank sent this.'

In another school, the play opened in the traditional fashion with Mary and Joseph setting off for Bethlehem. Joseph, a confident little boy in large glasses, spoke his lines clearly and loudly. Holding Mary's hand he gently led her across the small stage. Things didn't go

so well when the Innkeeper appeared. He was a sturdily built child with spiky ginger hair and his two front teeth missing. It was clear he had a number of family members present that afternoon, for there were adoring 'Oohs' and 'Aahs' whenever he opened his mouth.

Before Joseph could even enquire whether there might be room for them at the inn, the little bruiser, arms folded tightly over his chest and chin jutting out like a miniature Mussolini, announced: 'There's no room!'

'But we have travelled far and –' began Joseph.

'There's no room,' repeated the Innkeeper even louder.

'But –' started Joseph.

'Did you not hear me?' the cross Innkeeper bellowed. 'I said there was no room. You can go round the back, in the barn.'

'A barn?' repeated Mary. 'We can't go in a barn.'

'There's nowhere else,' said the Innkeeper. 'Take it or leave it.'

At this point the little boy caught sight of an elderly woman in the middle of the front row. It was obviously his granny. He gave a huge gap-toothed grin and tinkled the air with his fingers. The old lady, rather unhelpfully, smiled and waved back. This continued for what appeared an age.

'Shane!' came the teacher's disembodied voice from offstage. 'Shane! Come off!'

The Innkeeper continued to smile and wave. The voice from the wings was now more insistent. 'Shane Merryweather, get off that stage right now!'

The child was finally prevailed upon to exit stage left but did so with a flourish, smiling and waving, like a famous actor receiving the plaudits of a smitten audience.

Things then went smoothly until the arrival of the Three Kings.

'I bring you gold,' said the first child, laying a small golden box at Mary's feet and bowing low.

'I bring you myrrh,' said the second, laying a coloured jar at Mary's feet and bowing low.

'And I bring you frankincense,' said the third

King, rather dropping the gift on to Mary's feet. He then shuffled towards the side of the stage.

'Bow!' came the disembodied voice from the wings. 'Bow!'

The third King looked perplexed. He stared around him, seemingly frozen to the spot.

'Jason!' came the voice again. 'Bow! Bow!'

The little boy looked first at the audience and then at Mary. 'Woof!' he barked. 'Woof! Woof!'

18

The Journey to Bethlehem

All was now ready at St Helen's and here the Christmas play was staged rather differently. Mrs Smith, the Headteacher, explained that she had asked the children to write the different parts of the Christmas story in their own words and four of the best readers would read the narrative while the other children mimed the actions.

Mary sat centre stage, staring innocently

into space. The first little reader began the story: 'Long, long ago there was a girl called Mary and she lived in a little white house with a flat roof.'

Then the angel appeared, a large boy wearing what looked like part of a sheet with a hole cut in it for his head. He stretched out his arms dramatically as the reader continued: 'One day, God sent an angel and he told Mary she was going to have a very special baby boy and His name would be Jesus.' The angel looked heavenwards. 'When the angel went back up to God, he said, "Mary did what I commanded, God. She is calling Him Jesus, just as you told me to tell her."'

A beaming little boy with red cheeks strode

into the scene and positioned himself behind Mary, who was still gazing serenely into the middle distance. He put a parcel on the floor, then placed his hand on Mary's shoulder and stroked her fair hair.

A second reader took over: 'In a town called Naz'reth, there was an old man called Joseph and he was a carpenter.' The angel appeared again and stretched out his arms. 'God sent an angel to him as well and told him to marry Mary. So Joseph asked Mary to marry him and she said, "Yes please," and soon expected the baby. Joseph came home from work and he brought Mary some baby clothes and a big box of chocolates.' Joseph bent down, picked up the parcel and dumped it in Mary's lap.

Three children shuffled on, followed by a fourth smaller child pulling a toy sheep. The reader continued: 'In the fields there were these shepherds looking after their sheep.' The angel appeared again and stretched out his arms. 'The angel went to see them as well. When they saw this great shining light, they were really, really scared. "Ooohoo – er, ooooh – er," they went. "What's that?"

'"Don't be frightened," said the angel. "I bring you tidings of great joy. Today, a little baby boy will be born and you have to go and see Him." "Righto," said the shepherds.'

Three more children then appeared, staring upwards and pointing, at which stage a rather large girl pushed the second reader out of the way, and started to read: 'The Three Kings were very rich and they wore beautiful clothes and had these crowns and things. They looked at the stars every night. One night one of the Kings said, "Hey up, what's that up there, then?" "What?" said the other Kings. "That up there in the sky? I've not seen a star like that one." The star sparkled and glittered in the blue sky. "You know what?" said another King. "It means there's a new baby king been born. Shall we go and see Him?" "All right."'

The narrator continued: 'They shouted to their wives: "Wives! Wives! Go and get some presents for the baby king. We're off to Beth'lem to see Him." "Righto," said the wives.'

The Three Kings wandered around for a moment before miming knocking at a door. An aggressive-looking boy, with short spiky hair and a front tooth missing, emerged, holding a plastic sword. He stuck out his little chin and glowered.

'The Three Kings came to this big palace,' continued the reader. 'It was covered in expensive jewels and had a golden roof and a silver door. They could hear this blasting music. They knocked on the door and a man called Herod answered the door. "What do you want?" he shouted at them. "We are looking for the new baby king." "Well, He's not here!" said Herod. "And shift those camels. They can't stay there." He waved his sword about and said, "Clear off!" Herod was not a very nice man at all.'

At this point, a small boy wearing trousers too big for him replaced the reader. Mary and Joseph reappeared, pulling behind them a cardboard donkey on small wheels; it had a straw tail and very large polystyrene ears.

'Mary and Joseph went to Beth'lem on a donkey,' piped the small reader, 'but there was no room in the inn so they had to stay in a barn round the back. Mary had her little baby and she wrapped Him up nice and warm and kissed Him and called Him Jesus, just as God had told her to.'

Children began to enter slowly and gather around the baby. 'And from the hills came the shepherds and from Herod's palace came the Three Kings following a big star, and they all loved Baby Jesus. He was small and cuddly and He laughed. "Why is He laughing?" asked the shepherds. "Because God's tickling Him," said Mary.'

Last of all came the little shepherd boy and he laid the toy sheep before the manger. 'And they sang a lullaby for the Baby Jesus, and everyone was happy,' read the small boy.

The whole area was now filled with children singing 'Away in a Manger' in clear, high voices.

When the carol finished, I sat for a moment and looked around me: the children's faces were glowing with pleasure, Mrs Smith was wiping away a tear, the lights of the fir tree

winked and twinkled, and the walls were ablaze with the colours of Christmas. Through the classroom window a pale sun cast a translucent light and the whole world gleamed.

This was indeed something spiritual.

19
Christmas Eve

Christmas lights twinkled in the shopping arcade
That Christmas Eve.
Giant plastic Santas smiled
And mud-brown reindeers pranced across the
  walls.
Tinny voices of taped carol singers filled the
  air.
People rushed and pushed,

Hurried and scurried
To buy the last of the Christmas presents.

And on a bench,
Before the crib,
Sat an old woman
In shabby coat and shapeless woollen hat,
Clutching an empty threadbare bag
Smiling at the little plaster figure of the
  Son of God.

20

A Yorkshire Nativity

❄

With each season this vast, beautiful Yorkshire landscape changes dramatically but it is in winter that the most spectacular transformation takes place. It is then that the multicoloured canvas of pale green fields and dark fells, twisting roads and endless silvered walls, clustered farmsteads and stone cottages, squat churches and ancient inns is enveloped in one endless white covering, and a strange, colourless world stroked by silence emerges.

It was on a bright, cold morning, a week before the schools broke up for the Christmas holidays, that I went to Staplemoor Primary School and met William again. The last time I had visited the school it had been on a mild autumn afternoon. Gone now were the brilliant autumnal colours, the golden lustre of the trees, the thick carpet of yellow and orange leaves and the rusty bracken slopes. Now it was a patchwork of white, criss-crossed with the stone walls. The scene was magical.

I had met William, a round-faced boy of about ten or eleven, with apple-red cheeks, a thatch of black hair and a ready smile, on the previous occasion and remembered him as a very likeable and forthcoming young lad.

He now presented himself to me with a broad grin. 'Mester Phinn, in't it?' he said.

'That's right,' I replied.

'Schoil hinspector.'

'You remember me?'

'Oh, aye. Once met, never forgotten. I've a good memory for faces. How's tha doin'?'

'I'm fine, thank you, and what about you?'

'Champion,' he replied.

'And looking forward to Christmas?'

'Aye, cooarse I am. Best time o' year is Christmas.'

'And what do you like best about Christmas?' I asked.

The boy sucked in his lips and folded his arms. 'There's summat special abaat it, in't there?' he said. 'People smile more, they look 'appier. All t'shops are colourful and bright. I can't think what I likes the best. I love it in t'kitchen watchin' mi mam start baking 'er puddings and cakes an' mince pies an' I can sit

in front o' fire scraping t'bowl out afterwards. I like it when me an' mi dad go up to Durdeyfield Farm to get a gret big fir tree an' we purr it up an' me an' mi sister decorate it. Then t'turkey and t'goose arrive ready for pluckin'. That's my job, that. And if it snows, we all gu sledgin' down Ribbon Bank. Then on Boxin' Day, we watch 'unters and 'ounds 'ammering along 'igh street goin' to t'meet. Aye, it's a grand time o' year is Christmas.'

'I remember thinking the last time we met, William, what a bright and confident lad you were,' I told him.

'Aye, well, I think I told thee then, Mester Phinn, that mi granddad says not to be backwards in comin' for'ards. "Allus speak tha mind. Say what tha's got to say an' then shur-rup." That's what he says.'

'Wise words,' I said.

'Come Christmas mornin', we'll all be 'earin' 'im preachin' at t'chapel in t'village. I think I towld thee 'e's a Methodist lay preacher last time tha were 'ere. I reckon 'e's every bit as good as what John Wesley was. I love to 'ear mi granddad tellin' t'Christmas story. 'E allus tells it in 'is own way, Yorkshire fashion.'

'I've never heard the Christmas story told in the Yorkshire fashion,' I said. 'Perhaps you would like to tell me.'

'Ay, all reight,' he replied. 'I've 'eard it offen enough but it's worth repeatin'.' Then, cough-ing dramatically, the boy began.

'It were reight cowld that neet when Mary an' Joseph arrived at t'inn. "No room!" said t'Innkeeper. "Thas'll aff to gu raand back in t'barn 'cos we're full to bustin', what wi' all fowk comin' to pay their taxes. It's not too bad

in t'barn, it's warm and dry an' out of t'cowld an' I'll fetch thee a couple o' blankets round when tha's settled in." So Mary and Joseph went round t'back an' into t'barn an' med best on it. Meanwhile, in t'fields nearby were these shepherds watching ovver t'sheep. All on a sudden, a reight bright light shines down on 'em. "Hey up," says one of t'shepherds, "what's to do?" Theer stood this hangel, wi' wings o' fire an' an 'alo round 'is 'ead. Way, they were freetened to deeath were shepherds an' med ready to mek a dash for it. "Hold up," says t'hangel, "there's nowt to be frit abaat. I'm not gunna 'urt thee. I've summat to tell thee. I've cum down to earth to bring thee reight good tidings," an' then 'e tells 'em abaat babby what's been born that neet in Bethli'em. "Let's gu and see 'im," says one o' t'shepherds. An' so away they went, leaving t'sheep to fend for theselves. While all this were goin' on, there were these three Wise Men following yonder big star what sparkled in t'dark sky. After a bit of travellin', they came to a champion palace an' inside were a very nasty piece of work called 'Erod. "We're lookin' for a babby king," t'Wise Men told 'im. "Hast seen 'im?" "Nay," says 'Erod, "'e's not 'ere, but appen if tha finds this babby king, come back an' tell me, will tha?" He 'ad it in 'is 'ead to kill that babby. "There's only gunna be one king round 'ere," he towld 'imself, "an' that's gunna be me. Mek no mistake abaat that." Soon enough, shepherds an' Wise Men arrived at Bethli'em an' they found Babby Jesus layin' in a manger. "By the heck, 'e's an 'andsome little feller," said t'shepherds. "'E is that," said t'Wise Men, "an' I'll tell thee what, things are gunna change around here from now on. This little un layin' in t'manger's gunna light up people's lives like that yonder bright star in t'sky." And wi' that, they all knelt dahn before that little babby an' worshipped 'im, for 'e were t'Son of God, t'light o' world.'

The boy, who had been staring out of the window while he had related this astonishing story, licked his lips, wrinkled his nose and then looked up at me. 'Tha knaas, Mester Phinn,' he said thoughtfully, 'mi granddad says

that people sometimes forget t'real meanin' of Christmas. It's nowt to do wi' presents an' food an' such, he says. It's abaat that little babby in a cowld dark barn wi' nowt but t'bits of cloth what 'e were wrapped up in. Specially at Christmas, we should be thankful for what we've got an' remember them what have nowt. That's what mi granddad says.'

'Wise words,' I said again.

On that cold, raw December day, when a watery winter sun pierced the high feathery clouds making the snow glow a golden pink, and when the air was so icy it burnt my cheeks and ears, I stood at the gates of the school for a moment. I looked down on the panorama of

white, the deep valleys with long grey farmhouses, the meandering river, the omnipresent
sheep, the endless limestone walls, and I felt
glad to be alive.

I know that many of my stories are already used as readings during Christmas carol services across the country, and I am delighted about this. However, might I ask that readers make a small contribution to one of the two charities that I particularly support, CAFOD or Childline?

Thank you – and happy Christmas!

GERVASE PHINN

THE OTHER SIDE OF THE DALE

Gervase Phinn is offered the position of County Inspector of Schools in North Yorkshire because of his good sense and lack of pretension. As he reveals in this warm and humorous account, his first year was quite an educational experience.

He quickly learns that he must slow his pace, and spend time appreciating the glorious Dales countryside – 'Backwatersthwaite's been theer since time o' Vikings. It'll still be theer when thee finds it.' He meets some larger-than-life characters, from farmers to lords of the manor, from teaching nuns to eccentric caretakers. And best of all, he discovers the endearing and disarming qualities of the Dales children, including the small boy who, when told he's not very talkative, answers: 'If I've got owt to say I says it, and if I've got owt to ask I asks it.'

OVER HILL AND DALE

'Miss, who's that funny man at the back of the classroom?'

So begins school inspector Gervase Phinn's second year among the frankly spoken pupils of North Yorkshire. He finds himself confronting Mr Swan, whose hunger for his lunch exceeds his appetite for English; unwittingly plays the stooge to Mrs Peterson's class of juniors, and is alarmingly disarmed by a pupil unsure whether he is learning French or German.

But Gervase is far from daunted. He is still in pursuit of the lovely headteacher of Winnery Nook School, Christine Bentley; he is ready to brave the steely glare of the officious Mrs Savage, and even feels up to helping Dr Gore organize a gathering of the Feofees – just as soon as someone tells him what they are.

This is a delectable second helping of hilarious tales from the man who has been dubbed 'the James Herriot of schools'. It will have you laughing out loud.

GERVASE PHINN

HEAD OVER HEELS IN THE DALES

'Could you tell me how to spell sex, please?'

Gervase Phinn thought he'd heard just about everything in his two years as a schools inspector, but a surprising enquiry from an angelic six-year-old reminds him never to take children for granted.

This year, however, he has more important things on his mind besides schools. His impending marriage to Christine Bentley, the prettiest headteacher for miles around, finding themselves somewhere to live in the idyllic Yorkshire Dales, and the chance of promotion, all generate their fair share of excitement, aided and abetted as usual by his colleagues in the Inspectors' office. But it's in the classroom where Gervase faces his greatest challenge – keeping a straight face as teachers and children alike conspire to have him – and us – laughing out loud.

UP AND DOWN IN THE DALES

Now in his fourth year as an Inspector for English in the Yorkshire Dales, Gervase Phinn still relishes visiting the schools – whether an inner-city comprehensive fraught with difficulties or a small Dales primary school where the main danger is one of closure. With endless good humour, he copes with the little surprises that occur round every corner.

Some things never change, however: Mrs Savage roars, Connie rants, and Gervase's colleagues in the office play verbal ping-pong. But all this can be put behind him each day when he returns home to his lovely wife Christine, who is expecting their first baby. One day, their child will surely take the limelight in the local primary school where the children's contrived innocence never fails to win over even the hardest heart.

GERVASE PHINN

If you enjoyed this book, there are several ways you can read more by the same author and make sure you get the inside track on all Penguin books.

Order any of the following titles direct:

0140275428	THE OTHER SIDE OF THE DALE	£8.99

'The James Herriot of schools…Gervase Phinn writes warmly
and with great wit' *Sunday Express*

0140281290	OVER HILL AND DALE	£8.99

'A natural storyteller, he combines the timing of a professional comedian
with the palpable warmth and the ability to deliver a message that is much
more than just a series of jokes' *The Times Educational Supplement*

014100522X	HEAD OVER HEELS IN THE DALES	£8.99

'Uproarious and touching by turns, Gervase Phinn writes with enormous
warmth and wit about his romantic adventures, career struggles and the
children in the schools he visits' *Daily Mail*

0141011319	UP AND DOWN IN THE DALES	£7.99

'Phinn writes with that smooth, deceptively easy fluency which is the
hallmark of quality. Combine this with a seemingly inexhaustible fund of
anecdotes, peopled by characters brought to life with warmth, humour and
affection, and the result is as delightful as it is inevitable' *Yorkshire Evening Post*

Simply call Penguin c/o Bookpost on **01624 677237** and have your credit/debit card ready.
Alternatively e-mail your order to **bookshop@enterprise.net**. Postage and package is free
in mainland UK. Overseas customers must add £2 per book. Prices and availability subject
to change without notice.

---

*Visit www.penguin.com and find out first about forthcoming titles, read
exclusive material and author interviews, and enter exciting competitions.
You can also browse through thousands of Penguin books and buy online.*

IT'S NEVER BEEN EASIER TO READ MORE WITH PENGUIN

---

*Frustrated by the quality of books available at Exeter station for his journey back to
London one day in 1935, Allen Lane decided to do something about it. The Penguin
paperback was born that day, and with it first-class writing became available to a mass
audience for the very first time. This book is a direct descendant of those original
Penguins and Lane's momentous vision. What will you read next?*